LIVE DEAD

Live Dead is committed to planting churches among every unreached people group. We do so in teams that are multiagency, multinational, and multigenerational. Although Live Dead was started and is now stewarded by Assemblies of God World Missions (USA), we know and believe that Christ's commission is best obeyed in legitimate partnership with all the body of Christ.

Live Dead has three core values: Abiding (intimacy with Jesus through extravagant time in His presence reading the Bible and praying), Apostle (taking the gospel where the gospel has not gone, focusing on making disciples among all peoples and forming those disciples into indigenous churches), and Abandon (living a cruciform life by dying to self on a daily basis and paying any price to see Jesus glorified among all peoples). Teddy Hodgson and the missionaries that will be featured in future comic books lived out these values long before us, and we aim to follow in their steps with the empowering help of the Holy Spirit.

If, after reading this comic book, your heart burns with passion to glorify Jesus among the unreached and you want to participate through giving, praying, going, or a combination of the three, visit livedead.org for more information.

Dick Brogden
Saudi Arabia, 2020

SCOTLAND

Edmund "Teddy" Hodgson was a British missionary to the Belgian Congo in Africa from 1920 to 1960. He served Jesus and his church as a preacher, teacher, doctor, dentist, carpenter, hunter, husband, father, and friend. Ultimately, he was a martyr for the gospel of Jesus Christ.

IRELAND

◉Preston

ENGLAND

UNITED KINGDOM

Teddy Hodgson was born in 1898 in Preston, England. He left school when he was 13 and worked as a delivery boy for a bakery.

Soon he discovered that he was gifted to work with his hands, so he became an apprentice to a cabinetmaker.

Africa

Congo

At the same time, he met students at a Bible school and a pioneer missionary to the Congo.

After receiving the baptism in the Holy Spirit and admitting his love of adventure, Teddy promised God he would consider serving in the Congo.

Hodgson enlisted in the British Armed Forces while he was still a teenager and he served on the frontline in France in World War I.

The other soldiers called him "Holy Hodgson" and they respected his natural ability as a marksman and his fearless leadership.

Following orders to move out into no-man's land, Teddy was hit by a German shell.

He recovered but found his trigger finger useless.

After the war, Hodgson returned to England to start again. Driven and capable, he soon built a thriving furniture restoration business.

OPEN

There were times when the Congo crossed his mind, but having seen enough suffering on the frontlines of war, he believed he could serve God better by making money to give to missions rather than going himself.

Then one day the missionary he met before the war walked into his shop, and the missionary asked,

"Well, Teddy, what about the Congo?"

Over the next few days, a battle as fierce as anything he experienced in France took place in his heart.

He wrestled with the sacrifice it would mean for him as a young man to leave a promising business and disappear into the darkness of Africa.

However, when he finally surrendered to God, it was complete.

"Yes, Jesus, I will go to the Congo for You!"

Teddy said "yes" to God and never looked back.

Teddy sailed to the Congo in 1920...

UNITED KINGDOM

...and then had to walk the final 150 miles through mosquito-infested swamps.

AFRICA

CONGO

Within a week, he had malaria, and after nine months of pain he was nearly blind. He argued with God about bringing him to the Congo and leaving him useless.

Finally, in desperation, he cried out,

"Lord, either heal me or take me to heaven."

The next day, he was able to get out of bed and he packed his bags to go into the villages to begin his work.

Though he could not speak the Kiluba language well, Hodgson approached the village chief in Kisanga and asked to speak to the people. The chief gave him permission and he thought,

"Well, here's my audience so here goes!"

As he began to speak, he felt an overwhelming love for these people and the words seemed to simply flow from his mouth.

When he finished, he thanked them and left.

As he was leaving, two boys who were helping him build his house in Kisanga followed him and they were laughing.

They said,

"When you entered our village, we could hardly understand you. Your language is so terrible."

"But when you started preaching, we could understand EVERY word!"

Hodgson was really encouraged at this miraculous help that God provided, and this was the first of many times he found that God blessed and provided everything he needed when he made all of his resources available.

In the years that followed as he traveled from village to village, Teddy Hodgson had many frightening experiences with witch doctors, angry chiefs, hungry lions, rogue elephants, hippos, and crocodiles.

His trigger finger was useless, so he trained himself to shoot with his middle finger. Over the years, God used his ability with a rifle to win many friends in the villages. He killed more than 60 marauding lions, never shooting for sport or pleasure, only to protect the people he loved.

While serving in the Belgian Congo for 40 years, Hodgson's first wife died.

He remarried and his second wife died. Hodgson had to send his five children back to England for care and education.

These experiences hurt him deeply, but they also challenged his resolve. His love for Christ and the people to whom he was called compelled him to continue the work.

CONGO

KIKONDJA

In 1948, God sent revival to the little village of Kikondja.

As Christians prayed in the church, a mean rebel from the village stood outside mocking them.

Teddy and the local Christians had a special time of prayer for this man.

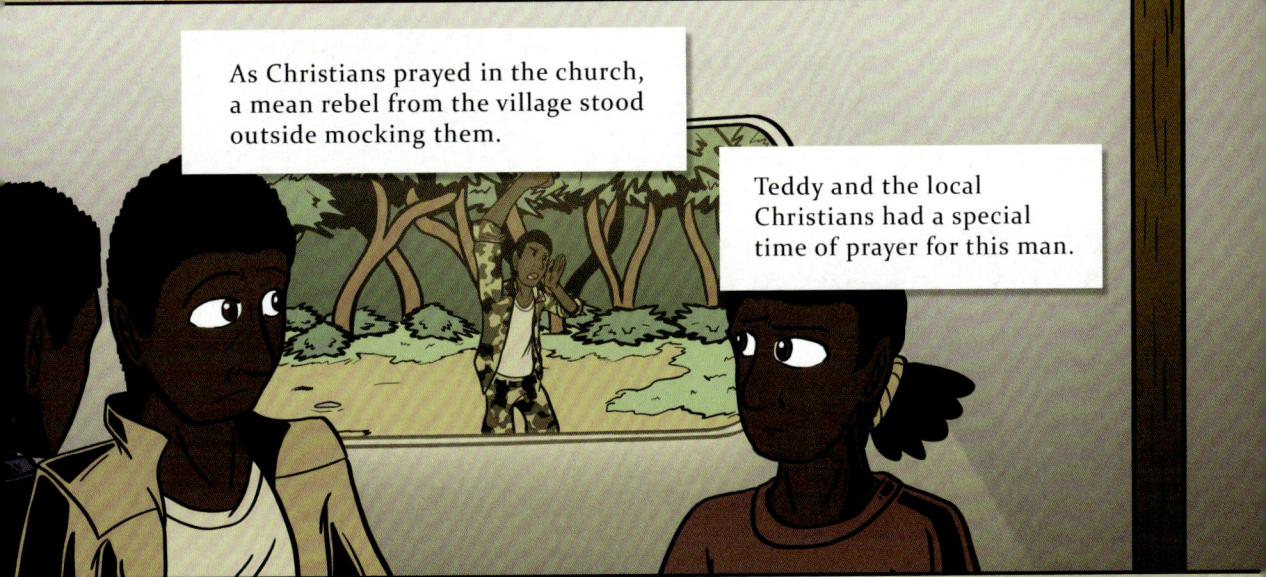

That very night, this man had a dream. In the dream God dangled him over the flaming fires of hell . . .

. . . and he woke up shouting for mercy.

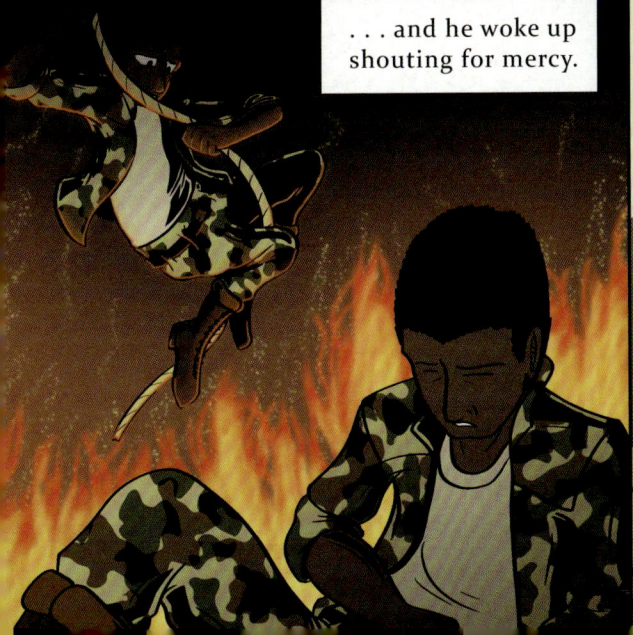

The next morning the local Christians found this man yelling again, but this time in the church. He was weeping and confessing his sin with groanings. Finally the man quieted down and said:

"God showed me how evil my sin is. He let me hear the cries of my friends who have died without Jesus. He told me I only have one more chance to repent!"

The repentant rebel begged the Christians to pray for him. They did and the Holy Spirit descended in a fresh way. The whole group was lost in praise and prayer that lasted six hours but only felt like a few seconds.

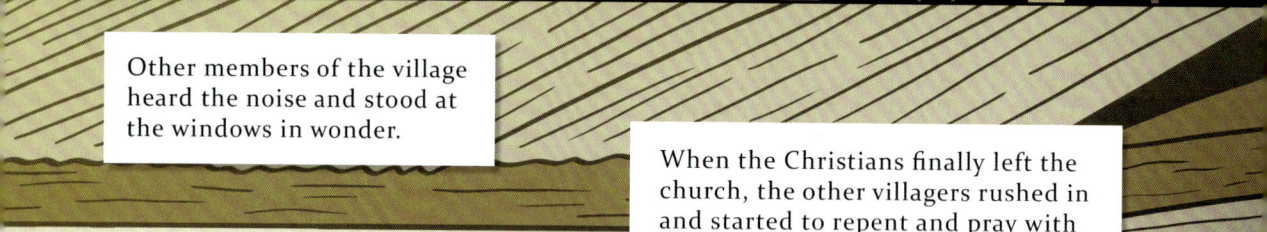

Other members of the village heard the noise and stood at the windows in wonder.

When the Christians finally left the church, the other villagers rushed in and started to repent and pray with tears for another six hours!

God met everyone that day in a powerful way, saving them and filling them with His Holy Spirit.

One of the men who met Jesus in a powerful way that day was named Peter. The day after this meeting in the church he was called to visit his uncle in a village 16 miles away.

His uncle, the leader of a secret Satanic society, had become sick.

The village was dark and demonic, and Peter felt the powers of evil so strongly, that he had to have a serious time of prayer before he fell asleep.

In his sleep, Peter dreamed that demons urged the villagers to kill him, and they tried to, but each time they tried, they cried out in pain saying,

"This man is protected by the fire of God. He is untouchable."

Peter woke up and discovered the villagers were indeed trying to kill him.

Though it was midnight, a heavenly light filled the hut and he heard Jesus clearly tell him in an audible voice:

"Preach the gospel, for behold I am coming quickly!"

Peter prayed for his uncle, and his uncle was miraculously healed.

The uncle and half of the village gave their lives to Jesus and burned all their satanic charms.

Filled with the fire of God for souls and with the command to preach the gospel ringing in his heart, Peter preached to every person he met on the 16-mile walk home.

As a result of God's people praying and preaching, 1,300 people came to faith and were baptized by Teddy and Peter and the other local Christian elders.

After the Congo declared its independence in 1960, the atmosphere changed for Hodgson and his fellow Christian workers. The missionaries soon found themselves contained in a small area in Kamina by rebels.

Teddy joined another missionary to take needed supplies to a hospital. They attempted to take the backroads to avoid the military checkpoints.

Teddy and his missionary friend were stopped by a band of surly rebels who were singing a song of the rebellion:

"We want no words from the white man's God!"

The missionaries tried to negotiate to leave the supplies at the hospital and return to their base. However, the rebel forces demanded they march with them.

A few Christians in the area heard about the trouble and followed from a distance.

After marching for a short time, the Christians saw the rebels stop.

They watched in horror as the rebels raised machetes. Hodgson and his friend Knauf were hacked to pieces before their eyes.

These two brave missionary men gave their lives so that Jesus would be exalted in the Congo.

Hodgson wrote in his book, *Out of the Darkness:*

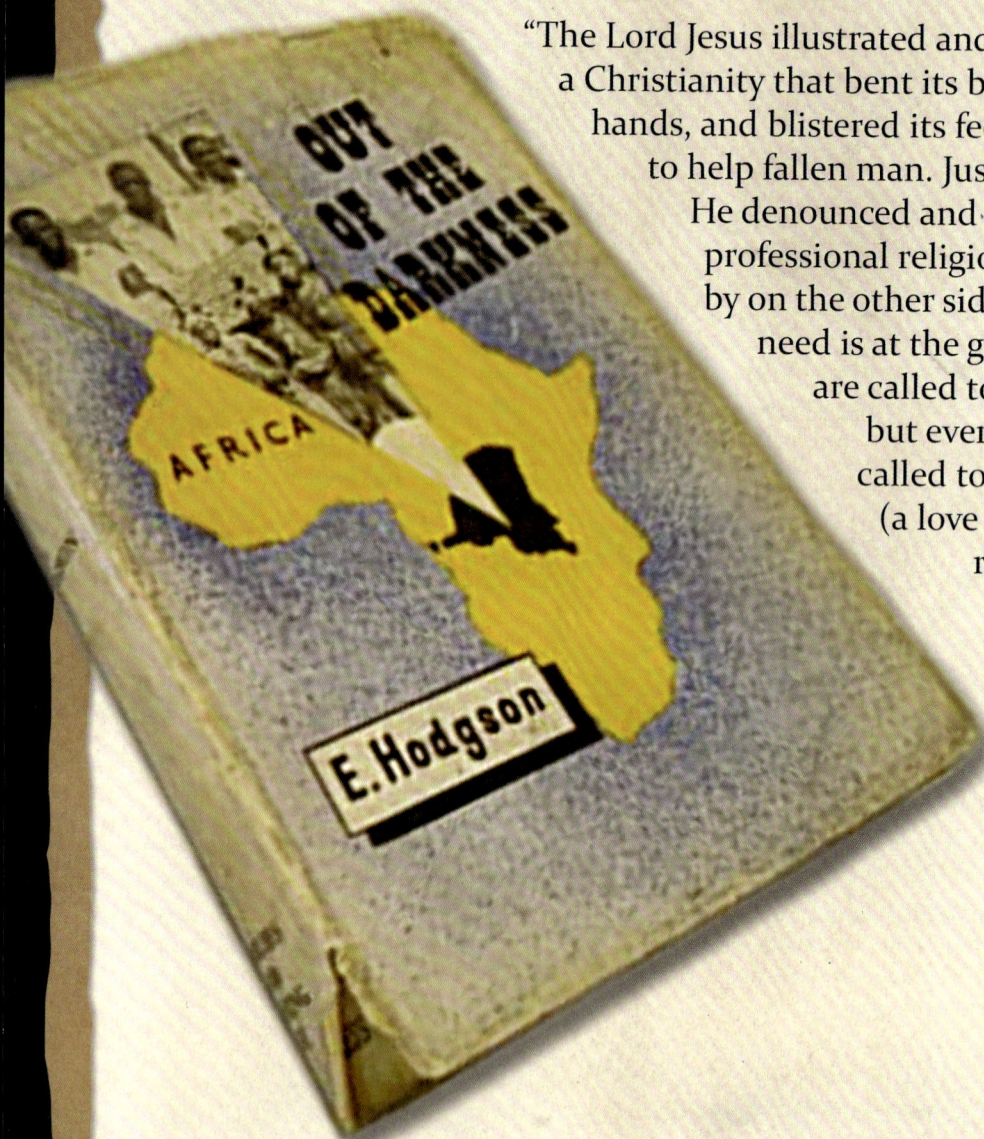

"The Lord Jesus illustrated and commended a Christianity that bent its back, soiled its hands, and blistered its feet in stooping to help fallen man. Just as positively He denounced and condemned a professional religion that passes by on the other side when man's need is at the greatest. Some are called to be Apostles, but every Christian is called to be an Epistle (a love letter of God, read of men)."

What we need today are more missionary men and women like Teddy Hodgson, men and women who will go to the difficult places and unreached peoples, stay there, and do the difficult things needed for revival to come.

It's not complicated. It's just praying and preaching, loving and teaching, and staying when things get tough. It's not complicated; it's just hard. But Jesus is worth it!